CARRYING ON

CARRYING ON
NEW & SELECTED POEMS
LEONARD NATHAN

UNIVERSITY OF PITTSBURGH PRESS

Published by the University of Pittsburgh Press, Pittsburgh, Pa. 15260
Copyright © 1985, Leonard Nathan
All rights reserved
Feffer and Simons, Inc., London
Manufactured in the United States of America

Library of Congress Cataloging in Publication Data

Nathan, Leonard, 1924–
  Carrying on.

  (Pitt poetry series)
  I. Title. II. Series.
PS3564.A849C37   1985   811'.54   85-40339
ISBN 0-8229-3525-2
ISBN 0-8229-5375-7 (pbk.)

The author and publisher wish to express their grateful acknowledgment to the following publications in which some of these poems first appeared: *Berkeley Monthly* ("The Scroll"); *Berkeley Poetry Review* ("Conversation Piece," "Haakon Jarl," "Hieroglyph," "The Poet's House Preserved as a Museum," "So?," "Twin Snakes," and "The Understanding"); *Bits* ("Sick Leave"); *California Monthly* ("The Servant of Stars" and "Toast"); *Cedar Rock* ("As We Walked" and "Season's Greetings"); *Chiaroscuro* ("Waving Good-bye," originally entitled "Revisions"); *The Chowder Review* ("Certain Prospects and Spectacular Diversions," originally published under the title "Diversions," "A Powerful Little Stove," originally entitled "The Solitude," "To Be Read to Yourself in a Public Place, July 4, 1976," and "To Transcend the Cat"); *Cincinnati Poetry Review* ("Just Looking, Thank You," "A Musical Offering," and "The Soundings"); *Epoch* ("Family Circle"); *Georgia Review* ("Carrying On," "Feeding the Ducks," and "The Fourth Dimension"); *Hawaii Review* ("The Lion Farm" and "The Chosen"); *The Nation* ("News from the Low Country"); *New England Review and Bread Loaf Quarterly* ("Explanation," "Near Things," "Surprise," "That the Unexamined Life Is Not Worth Living," and "The Third Wish"); *Northwest Review* ("Keeping the Faith," originally published as "The Law"); *Plainsong* ("Holding Pattern," "Icon," originally entitled "Iconography," and "Pocket Song"); *Poetry NOW* ("Body Count," originally published under the title "First Love," "Closure," "Creed," and "Yours Truly"); *Prairie Schooner* ("Hello Again" and "Morning Song"); *Salmagundi* ("Mocking Bird Song," "Thirty Rings," originally published as "Vows," and "Waiting Room Only"); *The Sole Proprietor* ("Opportunity"); *Windflower Press* ("At the Well," "Coup," "The Election," "Law and Order," "Letter," "Solemn Music," and "Tendril").

The poems "Gap," "Spirit," and "Widowhood" appeared originally in *The New Yorker*. Poems from *The Day the Perfect Speakers Left*, copyright © 1969 by Leonard Nathan, are reprinted by permission of Wesleyan University Press. Poems from *Glad and Sorry Seasons*, copyright © 1963 by Leonard Nathan, are reprinted by permission of Random House, Inc. Poems from *The Likeness: Poems Out of India* are reprinted by permission of Thorp Springs Press. Poems from *Returning Your Call* are reprinted by permission of Princeton University Press.

*The publication of this book is supported by grants
from the National Endowment for the Arts
in Washington, D.C., a Federal agency,
and the Pennsylvania Council on the Arts.*

For Carol

CONTENTS

NEW POEMS

Carrying On   3
Feeding the Ducks   4
Mocking Bird Song   5
Thirty Rings   6
As We Walked   7
The Poet's House Preserved as a Museum   8
The Lion Farm   9
Just Looking, Thank You   10
Twin Snakes   12
Body Count   17
Pocket Song   18
Surprise   19
Around the Fire   21
The Third Wish   22
Haakon Jarl   27
Season's Greetings   28
Certain Prospects and Spectacular Diversions   32
A Powerful Little Stove   33
Keeping the Faith   34
Concluding Remarks   35
Icon   36
Waving Good-bye   37

GLAD AND SORRY SEASONS (1963)

Learning Experience   41
Confession   42
The Diver   43
Wisdom of the Talmud   44
The Word   45
It Looks as If It Were Just Sleeping   46
A Reading of History   47

CONTENTS

THE DAY THE PERFECT SPEAKERS LEFT (1969)

Before Even This   51
Bladder Song   52
Progress Report   53
Outside the Wall   54
Niño Leading an Old Man to Market   55
The Loophole   56
The Day the Perfect Speakers Left   57
The Master of the Winter Landscape   59
Like Us, Maybe   60
Letter to the Patrol Twenty Years After   61
Nurse   62
The Highway   63

THE LIKENESS: POEMS OUT OF INDIA (1975)

Ellora   67
Snake Charming   68
Parade   69
The Likeness   71
Winter Morning of the Village   72
To Somewhere   73

RETURNING YOUR CALL (1975)

Breathing Exercises   77
One for Beauty   80
Sorry   82
Letter   83
Washing Socks   84
Pumpernickel   85
Jane Seagrim's Party   86

CONTENTS

Revival Meeting for Wheelchairs and Stretchers   87
Great   88
The Penance   89
Hay Fever   90
Honorable Mention   91
Audit   92

DEAR BLOOD (1980)

Gap   95
Widowhood   96
Opportunity   97
Evolution   98
Yours Truly   99
Creed   100
Hole   101
Family Circle   102
Tendril   103
The Election   104
At the Well   105
Coup   106
Law and Order   107
From To Be Read to Yourself in a Public Place,
     July 4, 1976   108
Letter   112
Kind   113
To Transcend the Cat   114
Closure   118
Hieroglyph   119
And Finally   120

CONTENTS

HOLDING PATTERNS (1982)

The Understanding   123
A Musical Offering   124
Meadow Foam   125
Table Talk   130
Near Things   134
Toast   135
Conversation Piece   136
That the Unexamined Life Is Not Worth Living   137
News from the Low Country   138
Morning Song   139
Holding Pattern   140
Sick Leave   143
Jubilee   144
Solemn Music   146
The Servant of Stars   147
Hello Again   150
The Chosen   151
Explanation   152
The Fourth Dimension   153
The Scroll   154
So?   155
Spirit   156
Waiting Room Only   157
The Soundings   160

NEW POEMS

CARRYING ON

At the next table, two carry on
over coffee and without love,
as another pair on the bridge whisper
softer than water and without love,
as a carp or shadow of a carp
idles deep in an umber pool,
at one with itself and without love,
and without love the doctor diagnoses
while the patient bravely hears and without it
the dog barks a warning, the pilot
safely brings down the wounded plane,
the dying hawthorn blossoms again,
and you tell me what has to be told,
and without love the law of gravity
holds, although I feel the ground
fall weakly away without love,
but without it much yet can be done,
and even peace be made, the peace
of knowing without love what needs
to be known, as the carp at one with itself
knows, or those two now going by
seem to know, holding hands
sadly for some reason, while darkness
swirls around their knees and the streetlamps
flare on like the round yellow eyes
of a huge night creature waking
without love to light us someplace
we have for too long avoided,
an empty cup, our very own,
waiting there for us to fill it,
a cat curled in the warm dusk
of a kitchen, dreaming without love,
waiting for us anyway.

3

FEEDING THE DUCKS

The person speaking now isn't
the person you think, and what life
has offered you as final isn't
just as this truth isn't the truth.

Under the great hackberry
on Putah Creek the ducks were receiving
crusts of bread that day, reflected
dully in the slow supportive waters.

Somewhere there's a saving fact
that is only what it is
and yet is just and merciful.
Do you doubt that? I doubt it.

Very few understand Einstein
but he, like Charlie Chaplin and Attila,
was one of us, not to mention
all other winners and their victims.

No other race can doubt and thereby
change the course of rivers, nations,
and end staring at institutional
walls, blind windows on nothing.

This proves nothing and is thus only
what it seems. It defends the right
of ducks and water to be what they are,
whatever they are, whatever we are.

About myself, I'm of two minds.
Saint Francis was one of us, but he
is dead. If you come to Putah Creek,
bring also a crust of bread.

MOCKING BIRD SONG

For years I thought the birds meant, well,
something, maybe because I'd seen them
only as movement, numinous,
in leaves or a blur in the blue yawn
of sky; and also the creatures rhymed
so perfectly with "words," thrush with hush.

I don't mean our kind of meaning—
imperatives for property
and sex, but reality if the brain
didn't shutter it. Note how we force
the least sparrow to signify,
even as it falls to serve our pity.

In the dream, Henri Bergson said
(in French so birdlike you had to be
a sparrow to understand) that this
was how he found it—reality—
watching *them.* A pane of glass
was suddenly snatched from between him and the world.

He swore he loved the flutter of it,
lying to save his reason. Think
of pure motion without purpose—
you can't. Even Hell is human,
desire without end, winged
and horny devils forking on their charges.

Note how the mocking bird is singing
stolen songs, as though for the hell
of it—that may be what is meant
by God, praise for simply being
without end. It's hard to believe.
And as for us down here, we know our duty.

THIRTY RINGS

He that made the vow under the fig tree
and she that bore him witness—where are they?
and the fig tree itself is now buried
in thirty rings of dead wood.

So we have learned—no more vows,
only habits and repetitions of names
for habits. Only the sweetness of real figs.
Truth then is a cry of surprise or pain.

That leaves all oaths and solemn pledges
to those who take words seriously and believe
they touch what they name. And who are those believers?
The innocent and, of course, the secret police.

A cry of surprise—See, a white flower
out of its season. A cry of pain—Look,
I've failed you again. You look. Yes,
that's all there is to it. And repetition.

But just before you turn your eyes away,
I see in them her, the lost one, buried
in thirty rings of the past. So we meet once more.
So nothing is ever lost, only betrayed.

AS WE WALKED

As we walked, I pointed, reciting trees,
and she nodded, but her eyes were filled with absence
like a remote country under clouds.
She was too young to care for anything
that served (like the blue called "sky") as background
for a face she knew would come to require
her close attention, while the rest of us would recede
into trees she'd forget the common names for.

If we could see the paths the birds have taken,
the air would look as worn out as the earth
in those smooth places lovers always walk
without seeing they walk in the steps of others
who didn't see because they cared so much.

THE POET'S HOUSE
PRESERVED AS A MUSEUM

Here by the fire, in his favorite chair,
he waited the coming of the Age of Spirit
with his friend, the philosopher, as his wife
stitched by the oil lamp on the oak table
and rain fell harder in the spring dusk
that darkened the wide window looking west.

He could, from this vantage, see far out
over the lake where the sun blazed through clouds
in a stupendous arrival of light just
before it set behind the head of his friend,
who was once more confessing the sin of doubt,
his huge brow bent helpless under shame.

The poet explained once more how all the signs
promised the Great Coming, but this time
his voice had in it something that made his wife
look up from her needle—It was the rain, she thought,
and the waiting and him so easily cast down,
but these were good times and there was tea.

Meanwhile, as summer swelled, the revolution
across the water became a bloody angel,
and one day his dearest sister stiffened
into wild silence, and then, also,
his friend, the philosopher, began drinking too much,
showing up in tears, his clothes filthy.

But visitors found the poet happy to tell them
the newer truth: that each must release the Spirit
within, though his wife could see that when he looked
beyond them west, he looked at nothing special,
and she could feel the pain of his favorite chair
as he sat himself deeper and deeper in it.

THE LION FARM

East of Los Angeles in a small town
called El Monte there used to be a farm
for lions, and on quiet days (and back then
days could be quiet) you would sometimes hear
a rumble like far-off thunder.

It faded with so many other dreams
after the Great War, replaced, I guess,
by small houses, leaving only in fall
a tawny shadow in the trees and the memory
of a noble fear caged.

This is the last harvest of that farm,
a few words on what its owners hoped
to raise—money by bringing home the beast
that could eat humans, who would pay to see
what time would do for nothing.

JUST LOOKING, THANK YOU

And when suddenly it hit me
that I would never get taller
or wiser or learn Greek
or Hebrew for a proper blessing
or prayer, never interpret
birds for humans or humans
for humans, never hear
the Word for Truth, never
get the first prize or be kissed
for courage, never be more
than the third (if that) person
to be contacted in case
of an emergency,
only a guilty bystander
who didn't get the facts straight
and who envied the truly good
and the lucky,
          I was not sad,
merely a little subdued,
feeling the spirit warmly
dissolve in my flesh like soap
in bathwater, and the food
placed before me then,
even the mashed potatoes,

became intensely personal,
and the stars over my head
unimportant except
as somehow necessary
to the local situation,
and the wars abroad something
to measure indifference by,
and you, the same as always—
turned sidewise with your own
occult obsession, and I felt
like a man in a hiding place
from the wind, or like a shadow
of a rock in a weary land,
secure in the dry lull
or depression between cause
and effect, for whom eating
mashed potatoes was OK,
and OK also allowing
the birds to mean nothing,
the humans to mean whatever
they mean, or so I believe
I believe—and just looking,
thank you, just looking.

TWIN SNAKES

Real are the dreams of gods.—Keats

Always for money, yes, and, yes,
to hurt whoever stood there waiting,
a reach away, to hurt him,
and yes, for the looks he got
by winning—cold admiration
in the eyes of women, even
his mother's—yes, for all that
and something more he couldn't say
but *was* the night he stood, radiant
with sweat, over a leathery man
he'd put down for the final time
and saw, like a vapor or spirit lifting
up from the smeared and slack stare
of the beaten other, recognition,
a swelling power that filled him
as his own hands filled the gloves
he held high over his head,
the same hands some fool of a writer
had called all flash and blur,
and another, twin snakes, yes,
the crowd chanting "Snake! Snake!"
as the police slowly wedged him back
toward his dressing room through waves
of fingers reaching to touch or snatch
a piece of him or his power,
and yes, after, out there
on the blurred and flashing street,
the girl on his arm, almost sick
with privilege, looking up to moan,
"You a *God!*" and he laughed, ashamed
for her, but knew he was, knew
he could make things be by thinking them,

12

be here: his ex-wife glittering
with regret, the blonde actress
who loved only the best, and then
the party in the rich hotel
where an old champion came up
and hugged him, whispering in his ear,
"I know," then stepped back, his arms
still wide, his suit too big,
his face gray as a man's a storm
has passed through or a fatal sickness
badly survived.
                    Next morning,
his own face woke him crying
out its hurt, but the girl slept on
as if she shared the bed with just
another man, and when he opened
the morning papers it was like reading
of someone else, someone whose fate
he followed closer than his own,
a much older brother or idol,
but more mysterious, whose every
least move revealed a purpose
beyond his power or understanding,
and whose picture in black and white
was calm as a mask and merciless
with a solemn concentration not his,
and he blushed when he read: "He goes at it
like a surgeon or a priest
of his own cult."
                    But the mirror showed him,
beside the bruised left cheek
where he'd taken a good shot, only

the same face he lived behind,
lived and still dreamed sometimes
of punching blind at shadows
on a smoky street, scared
of the darkness behind him, the fire ahead,
the same face he barely believed
was the one that millions saw on the small
blue screen and he with them
amazed at the pretty way he cocked
his head as if calculating
how and when the other man
would get it, how he slid off punches
and slid back in to deliver
combinations so fast
only slow replay could count them —
like a ballet dancer, he heard
someone say, no wasted motion,
only the grace to get what needed
doing done, and the twin snakes
he looked down at now, resting
in his lap like a pair of tame pets
he felt suddenly afraid for and wanted
to hide and hide himself.
                              It was then
he looked up, hearing her stir,
and saw her, yawning, open her eyes
and wave a drowsy little wave
as if this were normal and he the man
that did well enough what any
other man could do with her,
and he said, kidding himself, yes,
but furious, too, "I a god,"

14

but she laughed and yawned again:
"No, baby, *you* a man.
You bad but you a man,"
and there it was and all he could do
was laugh with her, but felt
inside—what?—a gray nothing,
or a weak little self hiding deep
in the cold and smoky dark he knew
he could dispel by letting in
the day—the praise, reporters asking
who was next and how it felt
to be champion, and yes, the money,
love and, yes, the show, but now,
under the smooth skin, the muscle,
there was nothing he could find or feel,
not even the little him
he was scared wouldn't escape
the dark, and he had to do something,
had to pull himself up suddenly
while she was in the bathroom, had to,
and had to pose that victory
again over the beaten man,
now a mocking absence below him,
had to lift his hands high,
to receive that swelling recognition,
but nothing came, except her,
so he had to pretend to finish a stretch,
and asked her if she was hungry, and yes,
she was, but so was he, human,
wasn't it?—to be hungry, human
to want something nothing human
could satisfy for long, so he called

room service, while she bent
tenderly above him, stroking the blue
and swollen bruise, whispering
when he winced, "Baby, you
a god enough for me," and he winced
again because that wasn't god
enough, not god enough in being
simply the best man, so he pushed her
away and started what was to be
a slap but midway turned to a soft
dismissive little pat on her cheek
because he was far ahead in his hate
to the next man he'd fight and who,
beaten, might not give him what
he had to be, the one who owned
a power not even winning could give,
could even take away, leaving
this poor love, money, and the show
of it, and knowledge like that
the old ex-champion had whispered
in his ear, an end he could now see
as if on slow replay, a fading
gray film, the figures shadowy,
moving as if in pain, moving
always slower, and then stopped
by her worry: "Baby, you alright?"
And yes, he was now, but jumped
at the light knock at the door
announcing what mere hunger required,
served by politeness on polished silver,
in white china so fine, he could,
without meaning to, have crushed it.

16

BODY COUNT

So many women are murdered because some man
failed with his first love, and so many men
failed with their first love because some woman
has not understood, and so many women have not
understood because some man has taught them wrong,
and so many men have taught wrong because no one,
not man or woman, knew the truth, and if
you lose count, go back to the very start,
a cold shadowy place before fire,
where a gene of loneliness tries to unite with a gene
of hope and the slightest miscalculation ends
in a present full of numbers laid side by side,
as lovers who failed, as bodies in a morgue.

POCKET SONG

Down in the dark cave
lives a poor family of keys,
a black comb with two teeth missing,
and a skinny knife, sharp as a pimp.

Every so often,
one of these is jerked up
blind into the air, used, then dropped
back down, none the wiser.

They make up little stories
to explain this, except the knife—
it lies on its side, rigid and folded
into itself, like a knife.

SURPRISE

The woman he thought liked him enough
brought a bunch of flowers home,
plain white marguerites,
for the oak table, the homely board
off which he ate, on which he paid
the bills, across which he gossiped and argued,
for that was the contract, burnt in the flesh
of the wood by a cigarette, in the flesh
of the mind by habit. Now and forever.

The woman he thought liked him enough
was leaving. There was a death in the woods.
The woods! A woman discovered stabbed
under the cedars, and in that death
was revelation, as in the plainness
of marguerites was a message inscribed
in a long-forgotten tongue, and besides,
she knew he was not charmed by roses,
but by plain habit now and forever.

He'd thought: Well, good, nothing more
could surprise him—catch him dozing maybe,
but not surprise him. Then she lit
a cigarette and, through the smoke,
said her good-bye. The flowers went off
like flashbulbs and the picture taken
was of a man with a foolish grin,
now and forever incredulous
before the truth, blurred as it was.

"Truth" needs another syllable
or two to get it right. Later,
he studied the flowers and found they also
carried their busy intelligent share

19

of alien life, eating out
their hearts and, of course, the bees had already
got their fill of them, and who
had ever asked us to dream the woods
were nice? That's nowhere in the contract.

But wasn't it these woods that bees
had mapped with lines running from sweetness
to sweetness, humming the silence? And now,
and maybe forever, he's sitting here
alone, a check for the rent waiting
only the habit of his name.
The life he thought was plain enough
is yet to be revealed. Meanwhile,
he fills the blank with what's required.

AROUND THE FIRE

Tell us about the wolves again—you know:
their tenderness to kind, their fine bearing,
their wisdom and respect for property, and how,
despite old stories, they kill only
to survive and to keep their part of the forest clean.

If you told them about us, would they believe it?—
How, anyway, would you translate "hope"
into Wolf or make them understand the idea
of solitude? How would you get them to see
that their world is merely the dream of a better one?

Tell us the part about how we mistakenly think
they're sad when their black silhouettes bay at the moon,
and how once you saw in tamarack shadow and snow
a joy beyond you and felt forever outside
and misjudged at the white fringe of a perfect system.

THE THIRD WISH

Simply the thing I am / Shall make me live.

The night her father asked her what
she wanted, she was amazed that wanting
was allowed, even a great wanting.
It made her cry, just like the time
she discovered stars—little stabs
of pure light—and asking
for a doll, knew already
that wasn't what she wanted
but would fill her arms awhile
as later offerings would, gifts
of sunlight and lilacs, a few friends,
a chestnut pony, music, and books
whose secret but true story always
arrived at a third wish, granted
if fatal.
   Each gift was stored
in a small room of its very own,
but there were other rooms to be filled,
perhaps larger, especially toward
the back, often approached in sleep,
where she heard behind one door
her father's voice, behind another
a strange calling she thought she should know
but woke suddenly to a dog moaning
in the next apartment.
     Meanwhile,
she bided the waste of her time
in offices, coffee shops,
museums and movie houses, watching
lives like hers distracted by jobs,
marriage, children, and the wisdom
of age, which is the old habit

22

that takes over when purpose goes,
when wanting sleeps dreamless
in the dark, one light, one year
after another extinguished or all
snuffed at once like the little candles
on a birthday cake, till even now
in the closeness of her own rooms
she felt surrounded by a black forest
of canceled possibilities,
one small lamp between her
and nothing, one lamp and patience,
so when the expected knock came,
she was prepared, opened the door,
and there he was, the very man,
or almost the very man,
violets in one fist, in the other
wine to match the rose tapers
she now lit, their jumpy flames
dissolving the walls in shadow
till the room became a cave—
nice, she thought, but already was thinking
ahead to where the tapers would sink
down in themselves and die, the plates
lie stained and empty, and he leave,
leaving her with only music,
and when that failed, her alone
with the one lamp.
                    It was then,
and still icily awake,
she knew it was time, knew the rooms
toward the back required her presence, lit
a candle stub and moved barefoot

into the dark, this time drawn
by something almost palpable,
like a breath on her cheek or the silence
after one last call, a silence
shrill with desperation.
                              At first
she passed familiar doors—the chamber
of sunlight, the room of close friends,
of lilacs, and nearing the back,
her father's unlit den where he lay
on white satin, his eyes still
staring up because, when most
it mattered, she could not bring
her hand to touch the cold face.
Finally she came to the last room,
the flame wobbling as she pushed
the door open and glided in,
seeing on the opposite wall
what looked to be a mirror, reflecting
her—no, no, not her,
a homely girl, almost a child,
eyes big with expecting, skin
and bones dressed for a party
in yellowed lace.
                      Impossible!
But then her whole life was,
impossibility waiting all
these years for what was possible,
what was even promised
by the very first gift, offered,
it's true, only as a token
of what was wanted but never named,

never imagined till now,
and her heart, refusing, flexed
and unflexed like a hand about to strike,
and then abruptly went soft and opened
because there was nothing left
except pity, not for herself,
but for what trembled as it approached,
begging forgiveness. So she blew
the candle out and took the creature
in her arms and rocked it, this thing
that would never speak, only shed tears
like those miraculous virgin statues,
except this one she could feel
dying against her, but as it weakened,
she grew terribly strong
as though a blind power were passing
into her life, preparing her
to do whatever had to be done
if anything could be done or saved
in this room or from this room,
which now began to contract in long
hysterical spasms.
                    Of course,
her first duty would be to bury
what she held, then to close
her father's eyes, and then, returned
to light, do the dishes up
as though to do this much contained
all the meaning required for doing,
for emptying the garbage, for all
else given her to do, patiently
bent to the thing at hand, a small,

accepting self which now renounced
all but the thing she was
after the final wish, and yet
not quite.
                    Something else
was in the room, something born
in the last and longest spasm, something
come forth full grown, standing
unseen behind her there, a powerful
second self, the one thinking
these very thoughts and watching the other
now as, say, a goddess might
observe the mortal she has been given
by birthright to protect so long
as there is life in it, watching
with impartial wonder the human
going on, doing anyway
without purpose, or some purpose
beyond purpose, like the simple
and obsolete animals trained to work
for nothing, not even a slap
of routine fondness; or like someone
lost looking cooly up
into the black socket of night
as though to take directions from stars
but nothing else.

HAAKON JARL

If the blue channel through the ice ahead
is the only way to go, we go. You were born
when snow was falling soundless on the water
and will likely die when snow is falling soundless
on the water. There are the cliffs through fog,
and through the fog your farm up in the stand
of pines, your woman in the steaming kitchen.

A slender ship is coming out of the fog,
red stripes on its white sail, and then
another and another out of the fog,
their timbers softly creaking. I then propose
we fight. I also propose there is nothing more
in all of this besides a certain knowledge,
a certain way to do what must be done.

And this is best. Summer melts in the hands
like snow. There was the warmth on your naked back
when you went striding down toward the great hall.
There was the girl who turned away as you passed,
the slender one, almost transparent in sunlight.
But you were born for winter, a grayness in you
nothing can ever touch or satisfy.

If anyone thinks about it, let him think
coldly of concentration hammered hard
as steel, of a certain knowledge ice allows,
sea and fog allow, and nothing more.
And you at the oarlock, as good as summer was,
you were not born for good. Now row. All
you have to understand is cold and hard.

SEASON'S GREETINGS

Waiting for the signal to change
in her favor, she saw him again
between sweeps of the windshield wiper,
the same man on the same corner
last Christmas, remembered now
because he was so wrong for seeing
this time of year in this part of town
where furs and jewels stared back
at one another in shop windows
that he passed unseeing and unseen
in a peacoat blotched and misshapen by age
and rain, himself blotched and misshapen
under a black stocking cap,
in one hand a brown paper parcel
tied with string, and now suddenly,
she was anxious—no, fearful,
because if life, her life anyway,
meant something (and she wasn't sure
it did), meetings as odd as this
might have some purpose, a sort
of repetition to make a point
she knew she wasn't getting yet
and didn't want to because now
she wasn't just fearful, but guilty as well,
and felt the petty cash in her purse
turn to ashes, the gifts piled
in the back seat become a reason
to look away ashamed, and then
it came to her—a vision—to her
who always saw in things mere things:
There was a box wrapped prettily
in shiny red foil, and in it,

she knew, was the future, its top torn open
to reveal a little room
with a cot, one rickety chair,
an old card table, on it
a dish and cup, both plastic,
and three black wire coat hangers
hung in a closet otherwise empty,
and the smudged window stared blindly out
on smoky brick—the right place
to meditate on soup kitchens
or on the intensive care unit,
but it was the honking behind that woke her
to this world where the man, whatever
he meant, had crossed before her, his eyes
ahead, his heavy face neutral
as worn stone that asked nothing
on its way into the darkening air,
and she saw she had the green light
to move, still shaken, to where
she must to get on home to the tree
the children had put up for her,
the grandchildren were now trimming,
and eased into quieter streets,
feeling boxed inside steel
and black traffic, driven below
by a power she never understood,
and feeling—well, sort of—followed,
and, glancing in the rear-view mirror,
smiled at her little panic, but drove
faster, recalling that this was the time
for exchanging gifts and she had given
that man (somewhere behind her) her guilt

(as if he needed that) so now
it was his turn, and she drove faster,
wondering with a cold thrill just what
he'd picked for her, and slowed down
when she saw ahead through rainy dark
another vision (her lucky day!):
Under the tree, almost buried
in glittering golds and greens and reds,
a brown paper parcel tied with string,
with her name on it, to be opened
the morning of Jesus' nativity,
and what it contained to be held up
in shaky fingers to her breast
(where her heart now worked unwilling
as a windshield wiper) to find,
of course, it was a perfect fit,
a garment made for her alone
centuries ago, and the man would be there
nodding in the corner, unseen
by the others—not really a man,
a thing older than humans, older
than Christmas, as though a stone or log
could, with terrible effort, take
our shape to tell us something, something
we had to know but didn't want to
because there was no remedy for it,
not even children (it was much older
than love), and she thought of all that ruin
of beautiful torn wrapping paper,
the afterbirth of giving, and saw
also she was simply home, parked
in the driveway, sitting motionless

to stare at the fragile strings of light
melting in the drops that ran
across the glass, and it was then
she put her head down on the wheel
and cried softly because she knew
the reasons for crying and knew too
that if nothing was saved of all the works
of joy, nothing would stop wanting
to be reborn, which made life
a kind of defiance. Yes. Well, then,
drying her eyes, she was ready now
to go in, ready to receive
whatever the children thought she wanted.

CERTAIN PROSPECTS AND
SPECTACULAR DIVERSIONS

The old man waiting bare-headed in the rain
for the last bus tonight is really my father.
He's waiting for sleep to pick him up and carry him
home, the last precinct of peace where children
eat meekly from his hand and his happy wife
and plump sisters make dumplings in the steamy kitchen
that warms the whole house. Heaven is like that,
a good dream of appeasable hunger, simple
as love that asks nothing but to touch. I,
meanwhile, am hurrying to the center of great beauty,
wit and power, a place of spectacular diversions,
and could seem, from certain prospects, to hope for too much
(which is Hell). And that's why waiting for the bus
in rain and darkness doesn't much vex my father,
but just thinking about it drives me crazy,
just thinking that maybe the bus will never arrive
or my own engine suddenly die in the suburbs.

A POWERFUL LITTLE STOVE

There's a solitude I fear but know
I want, like a small house in a village
in northern Sweden, snowed in
most of the dark year, but warmed
by a powerful little stove, like faith.

Old books on a sagging shelf:
most of a purely technical nature—
obsolete naval engineering,
some worn novels, and my favorite,
a child's history of the world.

I work at a story, my own, only
to make sense as the kettle sings,
and eat off a chipped blue plate,
and caulk every new crack
to avoid the thin lips of the wind.

You're not here, so I tell you snow
is as various of hue as your roses
or evil or love, so I renounce
all claims to knowledge excepting
this: Things won't be reduced.

Things just won't. They are too proud.
I have no radio, no mirror,
no mail service and still I hope,
waiting as though for revelation
but it's here, a snow of many colors.

This is a child's history of life.
Of course, I need you, and, of course, when you come,
all will revert to the old confusion.
A man in one of these books comes home
and doesn't know it, so strange are they both.

KEEPING THE FAITH

All around us things hold together
by a tense balance of forces, the lonely
negative side of one joined
to the lonely negative side of another, and all
without the slightest hope, as water
has no hope, or stone, but is faithful
out of necessity.

So when I read her letter a third time
and it still said no, I finally saw
that some marriages are made
in refusal devoutly forever and ever,
and the freedom given therein
is to love elsewhere and even often
but without necessity.

CONCLUDING REMARKS

The one before the Parthenon, before
St. Peter's, Chartres, and Stonehenge is you,
and you under those clouds that light falls through
like a radiant ladder to heaven in Tintoretto,
and here in your own garden, you want to explain.

You try words but are just now distracted
by a butterfly—two snowflakes
mating in midair—and the camera chooses
this instant to quote you, your mouth open
as if to say there's nothing more to say.

ICON

In the umber icon of a kitchen window
a woman's face mused through cold glass
as through layers of smoky varnish, the work
of an unknown master. And when we were called in
for coffee out of the leafmeal rain of a sun
steeped in distance, there was our cup, full,
and the warmth of this place fitted our skin like a skin.

WAVING GOOD-BYE

What I'm about to say should have been said
that night it rained all night at the shore
when everything else around was going under,
swamped by darkness and by water.

I told you instead about a man alone
on a raft in mid-Pacific—his radio
dead, how he began to talk to water
and lied to it and shocked himself.

I made this up. I made it out of silence
and desire. It was a time to go,
but something still required saying right.
I often talk to you when you're not here.

As I left, the sun lay fine and supple
on the hill, good light to go by
in a world wide enough to find
whatever needed finding still.

You waited till I turned to wave, and then
went in to have your second cup
and watch the copper pots slowly rekindled
by morning on the kitchen wall.

There was no turning back on the narrow road.
It smoked and shone. The radio
played a glad archaic music, noise
become a rainbow in the blue.

This is what I want to tell you—nothing
is the same. The hardest words

themselves revert to silence or dissolve
to syllables of rain. Good-bye.

This is what I really want to say—
nothing has changed. Consider the sun.
On the raft alone, I find I talk to water
and I lie. This is the truth.

FROM
GLAD AND SORRY SEASONS

1963

LEARNING EXPERIENCE

The sick sparrow, stiffening in my hands,
Died of itself five twitching minutes after.
How did I know it was so close to this,
And better left where, naturally, it lay?
I washed my hands three times in soap and water;
The dead bird in them would not wash away.

Cleanly blue and sun-showering sky,
Where did this fall from? Tender boughs of shade,
What do you hide? My children want to know,
Who never dreamt the world could hurt so much,
And, stricken by this petrifying stillness,
Find no comfort in my poisoned touch.

CONFESSION

In certain situations, replying nothing when asked what one is thinking about may be pretense in a man. Those who are loved are well aware of this.
—Camus

Emptiness in my eyes had begged her question:
    "What are you thinking of?"
And could I say, "At just that very minute
I'd made the earth a better place to love."

My potent hand, the first day of creation,
    Labored in gold and green;
A garden the second day, I strolling in it,
Handsomely at one with what I mean.

Then, on the third, the light-made-flesh, a girl;
    The fourth, her twin, but dark;
The fifth, with such alternatives to play,
I sampled all my lordly handiwork.

Yet on the sixth, a sense of cold uncoiled;
    We'll call it—well—a snake,
A deadly thing, but made in my own image;
The seventh was rest for its compulsive sake.

And then she asked the silence where I hid,
    "What are you thinking of?"
"Nothing," I said as I restored the void
And saw across it what there was to love.

THE DIVER

Tucking in yellow curls, she poises, set,
Then leaps to form so fine a diving curve,
I guess how Plato, making young grace serve
Unearthly need, brought forth Ideas. A jet,
Fanned out to crystal, echoes her proud arc,
Which, at the pool floor, ends in fluttering white,
Bringing from under bubbles into light
The Beautiful. I close my eyes till dark
When one low whistle is my sign to creep
To where she lies, and like a long-blind seer,
Feeling his way to truth, I then go deep,
Down that steep burrow, under musky fur,
Where captains of pure reason die like sheep,
To find this gripping earth alive with her.

WISDOM OF THE TALMUD

This is what those rabbis said:
"A ram, alive, has just one voice,
Seven after he is dead,
Exceeding the natural one in grace.
His horns make trumpets, guts the wires
To pierce the harp's framed air, the lyre's;
Hip bones make pipes, the skin a drum—
And all to prove death is not dumb."

There is so little left to waste,
The butcher having dressed the meat
And the gut, bone, and skin made new,
That only the windy breath and bleat
Prove useless in this fertile beast;
Yet seven musicians, playing true
Their several parts, could never gloss,
With all their skill, the sound of loss.

THE WORD

When I remember first it rhymed with breath
And dropped like a lid on wooden conversation,
As, hustling all the sobered kinsmen home,
It told the absence of some near relation.

When I remember second, O what a word
To mouth and threaten with, till you were kissed
Off eastward with a million kissed-off men,
Casualties of love; but what's a list?

And later, no word at all, no rhetoric
Of absence, love, no counter for the dying
To close the eyes on such a solid thing:
The word is flesh and there's an end to lying.

IT LOOKS AS IF IT WERE JUST SLEEPING

I thought in the sweet stink of the funeral parlor,
My skull, though whittled out of lead, would split
And then I'd whine or squeak or bark
Because the corpse, glowing like wax fruit,
Was smothering in condolences of flowers,
An awful job they must have done in dark.

For refuge in the paralytic hush,
I traced my black sleeve to its severed end
Where knuckles bulged a cage of bone
That locked upon another's bird-warm hand,
My wife's contagious tenderness of flesh
Which hung upon a shaken skeleton.

And was alone, though in official mourning,
The chaplain read that little, fathering psalm
Where lambs may have their green escape
By dreaming, beyond all shadow, kingdom come.
But posted by the coffin's overt yawning,
Who could make me trust again in sleep?

A READING OF HISTORY

The good guys lost the city first;
The bad guys never should have won that battle,
But did and turned the good guys out to starve
Or butchered them as they had butchered cattle.

The bad guys lost the city next;
The worse guys swarmed the walls from land and sea
Till heroes of evil parcelled out the widows.
O then how good the bad guys seemed to be!

The worse guys lost the city next;
Shaggy brutes slashed in from west and east
To drag them from their temples by the hair,
For worse guys were too gentle for this beast.

Yet who but this beast assembled later,
Three to a corner, stricken by whispered fact
That powers of darkness hovered off the coast
And nothing could prevent their being sacked.

The future plainly belongs to evil:
To good, the past; and for the present—well,
Good guys and bad guys mingle in the market;
Business was never better. Time will tell.

FROM

THE DAY THE PERFECT SPEAKERS LEFT

1969

BEFORE EVEN THIS

Green from the apple orchard farther west,
The wind shouldered the grass until it seemed
A tide mounting the hill where we two sat,
And April, you said, was just about to crest.

It was like seeing from its central throne
A realm so total there was ample room
For kindness like yours to counterpoise the hawk
Who dropped through blue attention like a stone.

On such good grounds, unscarred by praise or blame,
We rested. That was, of course, before the world
Had slept with winter, learned to count the change,
And got, among the stars, its evil name.

BLADDER SONG

On a piece of toilet paper
Afloat in unflushed piss,
The fully printed lips of a woman.

Nathan, cheer up! The sewer
Sends you a big red kiss.
Ah, nothing's wasted, if it's human.

PROGRESS REPORT

The trees won't talk; but we've got instruments
To get the truth. Old omens of the air
Mean birds are hungry, here as everywhere,
And speak, if forced to, in the present tense.
This took eternity and some expense
To verify. Gods, never really there,
Reduce to heroes dying for a share
In prospects disconnected and immense.

Symbols, like homespun drugs, were handy things,
But facts are good as guns. And then there's you—
No priestess circled by sacramental wings
From Cythera, but a girl well suited to the act;
And what's to be done with nature? Nothing new.
We'll dream in symbols, wake up cold in fact.

OUTSIDE THE WALL

There is a wall that runs right through the summer,
An adobe wall since summer is Mexico,
And in the shade of the wall the noon is rich.

As rich as sleep, as rich as time, as men
Who rest in it awhile and hear far bells
Upholding heaven with their high-born tongues,

Or, in a fluent native, jacarandas
Lisping minor instances of good,
Of good just now, of lowly nearby good,

Of one adobe summer stretching on
To where the bells are jacarandas shading
Wealthy noon forever in that land

Whose names for things are right, whose time, asleep,
Dreams of the risen poor astride the sun
On one long progress toward the walls of heaven

Which is Mexico and runs through death, right through.

NIÑO LEADING AN OLD MAN TO MARKET

He is leading his grandfather under the sun to market.
Who needs to see? The hand is warm on his shoulder.
The sun tells a man whatever he has to know
And the eyes of the children take care of the rest.

This is a little procession, solemn and steady,
A way of seeing that has the right direction,
And needs the simplest of eyes; the hand is quite sure,
And the wealth of the sun takes care of the rest.

His children have children to spare for any errand
An old man must go on; like sun, they are warmly with him,
Though at night his wakeful hand may remember that seeing
Was going alone in any direction.

Time takes care of the rest. In the niño's eyes
He is leading his grandfather under the sun to market.
In the old man's mind he walks through warmth where he must.
They are going in one direction, and know it.

THE LOOPHOLE

Any contract, tax form, Great Idea,
Existentialist brick wall,
Or even the cloudless air provides
Some saving orifice after all,
Through which, well greased, the lawyer, the statesman,
Or the fattest theologian can squeeze,
As can the executive and editor,
And with an almost obscene ease.
The motto over the loophole reads:
"Courage! The end wipes out all means."
God went through two centuries back,
His logic chopped by strict machines.
Peer through: theaters, suburbs, parks,
Factories, monuments, great stores,
A traffic problem. Which is which?
But you're on the proper side, of course.
Some have heard voices from that world—
Distorted, wishful, uttering facts
Terrible in their lack of portent:
Anyone's name (say, John) or acts,
Like loving when it seems to open
The ivory gates for you alone,
But closes, after sex is finished,
On something as alien as stone.

And beware mirrors, not that they open
To evil, but that they can show a face
That seems to look from the other side
Which couldn't be (could it?) so bad a place.

THE DAY THE PERFECT SPEAKERS LEFT

It was as though it had begun to rain lightly
On the amazed stillness of birds
And leave-taking was another,
Sadder version of dusk we were attending,
And as though a whole age were going out,
Its head covered, and going out with it
A purpose including stars and stones.

What were their last words
Before the gates shut and small lights
Moved slowly up the hill of dark?

We were to mean everything this once,
Include in what we meant the birds and stars.
The stones too, and be no more watchers
On far shores, on single peaks, listeners
In little rooms, for news of how it is;
We were to hear the true last names for things,
The utter ode, composing us at last
In the rounding music of our sphere.

The gates are shut, the lights over the hill;
The barest voice softens in rain,
Streams out in wind, alleges more in dark than it knows.

Their words are hard to say, hard
To remember when you wake at dawn,
The bare light alerting you to plainness,
Solitude of stones, terror in birds,
Stars drifting off, the feel of huge leave-takings
For which no name, the first or last, consoles.
How can you trust those hints at dusk
Of foreign magnificence?

It may have all begun with a few native words,
Good, but made grandiose by wind or sad by rain,
Our own weather, sparing us a vaster silence.

This is when I turn, trusting you're here,
To say barely what's left, a few last words,
As though leave-taking itself composed
A plain majesty—the way light moved
So slowly up the hill of dark, who held
The light, his special purpose, the grief of gates,
What can't be said, but must. This is to leave
Almost without words, as though dumbfounding
The perfect speakers by including them also
In a fitting good-bye.

And this is how stones are spoken for down here,
How birds, how stars, and the foreign mutterings
Of weather, and how men, and what they might mean.

THE MASTER OF
THE WINTER LANDSCAPE

This is that other place, north of the last
And most daring flight. Here, driven off course, small birds
Compulsively circle until they drop; the trees
Have marched against it, but always come reeling back.
No leaves, no song. Here, sun and moon are one:
A blinding wheel of snow or sometimes a shine
So pale it would ice the heart if the heart could feel it,
Could come to the middle of white within white and feel.

He, though, has been here, if only in wintering sleep,
Found himself present and breathed in that rigid air
Of no leaves, no song. Thus birds may now live here, and trees,
Though frail, bear the wind. And so we have peopled the place
With the ghost of a snow goose, the hint of a crippled pine,
Merely perhaps to say that here one man
Has stood for the rest of us to discover that nothing
Is just what we thought without us. And this is his mark.

Ready or not, we are natives now. Though it's cold,
Though the wind refuses our gifts, we know how to praise it.

LIKE US, MAYBE

These people discuss spirits as if spirits
Were leaves, or might be. They also hint that leaves
Are something more, maybe: like spirits, leaves.

A winter people, they are abstracted much,
Staring at the fire which, they say, is their guest,
A great prince, the sun, lost in the snow.

About pain they are simple; but all the rest they find
More than it is. They have listened to the wind
So long, everything seems strangely kin.

They are a people whose words, lifted by wind,
Take flight like spirits, a people like us maybe,
But poorer, whose leaves mean everything. And must.

LETTER TO THE PATROL
TWENTY YEARS AFTER

Remember Ralph who ran so fast and far?
Remember Frank who found the way through dark?
Remember Leo who never missed the mark?
And Nick whose hands could bend an iron bar?

Lieutenant Smith—can't you just see him yet?
Always out front, a natural leader, he.
I followed him with you. Remember me?
I am the one who never could forget.

French girls we swore to marry as a whim
Come floating up to mind; it's age I guess;
And are you others having much success?
The prisoner we shot—remember him?

Not since the Army have I held a gun.
I grow rare roses; that wouldn't interest you,
But men should have some different thing to do.
I'd like to hear what all the rest have done.

Lieutenant, still ahead? Nick, just as strong?
Leo, as steady? Frank, still on the track?
And Ralph, as quick? It's quite some distance back,
And who'd have thought one death could take so long?

NURSE

The day that she put on white for good
An apple blossom fell. The bee,
Destined for it, was never seen
Again. Forget apples and honey.

Pain is a kind of blossom too.
She lines toward it, almost unthinking,
Through the long straight corridors,
Bearing her sweetness in a sting.

When she enters, bends and touches,
Whoever has called her holds his breath.
Sexless winter snows the ceiling;
Forget time, forget even death.

Off duty, naked in the bed,
She hardly feels her man's caress;
The white love she has carried home
Numbs them both with tenderness.

And is the apple blossom a pain
The bee relieves, and is honey
A rich oblivion? She thinks,
Dressing for work, she does it for money.

THE HIGHWAY

In that town, the Golden Highway ended
At the newly built El Roy Motel
Where I was lodged for a single night's
Luxurious loneness; early next morning,
On a balcony that oversaw
A swimming pool glossed by a delicate wind,
I mused coldly on that green water
And the locked-up sleepers who later would warm it;
And when, in my used-up room, I repacked
And snapped shut the suitcase, the pool flashed
In my mind like a signal winking through sleep;
Through sleep also the truckers loomed on
Toward their coffee stops, towering by
In their tall cabs, looking down, alone;
And alone I left, but—with the high vigilance
Of truckers—took from sleep its warmth;
From water, its green-wind dawn; from going,
A way to leave without good-bye.

FROM

THE LIKENESS: POEMS OUT OF INDIA

1975

ELLORA

I was watching the great God dance
In the stony dusk of a cave
At Ellora, when all the beggars
I ever refused marched in.

They were terrible and endless and true
And they marched right into the stone
And they danced right into the God
And looked from His eyes as they danced.

They did not believe I was real,
Rich, yes, and strange, but not real.
They did not grant me my name,
And knew I could barely feel.

If God and the poor are the same,
Nothing can save the world;
It will go on dancing forever
For stone is always the same.

The poor are always the same—
That is the thing you can feel
Watching God dance in His cave.
It is cruel and hard to be real.

SNAKE CHARMING

Here It is: squamous, hooded,
Cold, slid from the mineral sleep
Of rock, of metal, come a long dream
Up the terrified trail of the warm-blooded.

The killing god is also a dancer.
Is there nothing human under the sun
But ourselves? We stare at one another;
Why is evil our ancient answer?

And we are ancient, heads cocked, every
Back hair needled up, one
Vulnerable heel hung in the air,
And the woods stiffened; a step away

The Other, what seemed a dead stick,
Lifted before our mammal eyes,
And we make, as it writhes toward us, silent
As God, this charm of minor music.

PARADE

She had climbed into sleep halfway
Through the *History of India,* riding
Virginia Avenue out to the stoplight
Where twelve abreast rows of Indians were flowing
From right to left down Oxford like a slow freight—
Rajas and maharajas in azure turbans,
In royal magenta robes, badged with sapphires,
Belted with onyx, jade-handled swords at their bellies,
Their ranis floating behind them, tiaraed in gold,
In opal, in topaz, wrapped in twelve silk yards of sari.
Bangles and anklets of silver, a salvo of bells
As they stepped with their great lords behind them,
With dewans behind them in white linen gowns,
The fat, the skinny, their chains of office, and rings
Like constellations of sparks as they fluttered their fingers,
And the rich in satin, brocaded in red, in yellow, in blue,
And the saints in a blaze of orange, holding brass bowls,
Or naked and holding tridents, ash on their foreheads and cheeks,
And the middling people in fresh bleached cotton,
Row behind row behind row till the poor came on
In homespun and dirty white, in deadened saris,
And more and more, and beggars gimping along,
Holding a rag at their middles, babies hung
At lank mud-colored breasts, one-legged men,
And no-legged men somehow twitching forward,
And the eyeless and the lop-limbed with sewn-up mouths at the
     elbows,
And the starving, already spirits, and their rib-caged
Knob-jointed, lizard-skinned children
Followed by lepers with noses like burnt-out stumps,

With a blackened stubble of fingers, with eyes that seem charred
Through layers of shock, and more and more—from hill,
From jungle, from village, from nowhere at all,
Always advancing, a fatally poisoned thing
That dragged on forever, and would not stop, though the light
Turned green then red, then green again, then red.
And she sent out cargoes of wheat to her right;
And out to her left, the money saved up for Christmas,
Five little gifts, a surprise for well-fed nephews;
And she threw her new gloves away, her lipstick away
And wired the U.N. for help and got in reply
A four-thousand-page report detailing the good
She had done, like the hundred doctors reeling with fever
As they issued, exhausted, the pill to seventy
Million women who thought it would bring them sons,
Like the computer's prophesy that Chinese still, Egyptians
Still were destined to march, or like news that the submarine
Just now crossing under the ice of the Pole
Had zeroed in and was ready, and news
That rains had failed, that yogic breathing had failed,
The *Gita* failed, that goodness got poorer and poorer,
And her duty was only to keep on concerned as they passed—
Now rajas again as if to start over,
And she suffered that progress as if trapped in the bones
Of a child till darkness woke her at four,
Where she lay now trampled and silent,
Vowing never to cross Virginia again at Oxford,
Vowing never to dream again of people.

The stoplight facing Virginia so early blinks red,
Oxford blinks amber, though no one is crossing so early.

THE LIKENESS

What is it like to have just one shirt,
To have no money forever, to have nothing
Pertaining to men, to begin in dirt
And to end in dirt?

What is it like? Dirt for breakfast,
Breakfast for supper, nothing that does not pertain
To misery, to arrive hungry
And depart hungry?

To have nothing pertaining to love or money,
Nothing not dirty and just one shirt,
To be so cold when the world is cold
That to breathe can hurt.

Nothing, I tell you! And what is it like?
They can never, ever, ever tell.
They squat by the wall; they won't go to school:
They will not rebel.

This is a rock. You can chip away
Till it looks like a man and it can't feel pain
And it will not hope and it doesn't want love
And that's all you can say.

WINTER MORNING OF THE VILLAGE

This village is so much smoke.
The houses are smoke, the people smoke.
A small fire here, a small fire there,
And the rest is smoke, even my eye;
It is hard to see through, smoke,
And the people think themselves solid,
But only because they are hungry.
In my smoky eye they are smoke,
In my smoky thought you are smoke,
My woman, and sweet, and hazy
And bitter, my friend, my reader,
Smoke. Smoke. They use cow dung here,
Waste paper, twigs, to get it going,
The poorest things for warmth, for light,
For smoke. And now it comes clear:
Smoke spreads as it winds into air
Into other smoke. That is our secret,
And it feels so true to be smoke.
What dawn blows away lives everywhere now
In the world. God may be so much smoke.

TO SOMEWHERE

This is the road to Somewhere—
All feet and all hooves
That take it, and all wheels,
Set out for something rare:
The water's source, beauty, riches,
Or one truth in God's many names.
On the way, flies for companions,
The skin, like a separate beast, twitches,
And men brush their streaming eyes,
But see no better through the dust
That cartwheels turn up in a delirious
Riverbed of swollen days.
Sometimes, its windows shut tight,
A royal car swerves by destined
For the beggar's black ditch ahead.
The travellers pass it at midnight,
Emptied of purpose, and they don't care;
They've forgotten all but going, forgotten
The goods that set them forth; in truth,
Forgotten how to stop, but will somewhere.

FROM
RETURNING YOUR CALL

1975

BREATHING EXERCISES

My mother phoning from far off:
How are you? How are you really? Really?

A long dumbness fills with breathing.
How much does she want to know? Really?

I'm fine, fighting, making passes,
Doing my job. Does that sound right?

No, it sounds as if somebody bugged
The phone and I'm talking for the bugger.

Which reminds me: I'm Leonard Nathan whose grandpa
Changed his last name—too Jewish.

I'm not Leonard Nathan. I'm hiding
Down here and have fooled the psychiatrists.

You know what I do? I breathe slyly.
It's nice to breathe, that's the spirit. ·

Wonderful. Inside Leonard
Nathan is a little spirit.

Rocks in the desert also breathe—
More spirits, and water breathes deep.

If somebody screws your mouth shut, whistle
Through your nose. For God's sake, keep breathing.

Inhale fifteen seconds, thinking
OM, hold ten, exhale fifteen.

Grandpa scares me holding his breath.
His last address was an oxygen tent.

My belly rises and falls, tidal,
But the phone ringing can freeze me solid.

Hello, this is a rock calling
From the floor of the sea, your great grandma.

Hello, this is an empty bottle
Calling from the desert: I'm going crazy.

Put father on. He's watching the Jets
Blow somebody right out of the stadium.

He breathes deep in himself, precious
To himself. Daddy's a real rock.

My son is inhaling a whole sky
Of filth. He hates telephones and ideas.

I ask, are you there? Mere breathing
Answers. That also scares me.

Listen, I'll breathe with you, inhale
For grandpa, exhale for a grandchild unborn.

Sometimes I get the cadence of things
And breathe with them, like music, but not.

They paraphrased Hsieh Ho: "The life
Of the spirit in the rhythm of things." Nope.

You can't paraphrase. You can't say anything.
You live in a tent deep under water.

And someone just stopped breathing again.
Grandpa, names change nothing but words!

This is a prayer to your absence. Hear me.
I lean close. I hiss. I breathe into you.

Out of the stupid air of the desert
I made it and the musculature of the sea.

It is so much wind, but I want it back,
Sucking it out of your life, my spirit.

My mother won't hear. She listens far off
To her self. That's how I am really.

ONE FOR BEAUTY

I tell Beauty, at Her most loving, to shut up.
I can't praise Her in all this racket.

Any one of nine sirens could be
For me, ME, and She wants praise.

I say: Look at the front page, you nitwit.
Life is too serious for this clowning.

She thinks She's Mae West, or Sophia Loren
Whispering *Caro, caro mio.*

Or Indira Gandhi cooling two hundred
And fifty million hot males.

Someday I'll tell Her it's not loving
She wants, but attention, all the attention.

The bread of the world can burn if only
We treat Her right. She thinks we need Her.

We. The men. She doesn't think much of women,
The silly bitches. They bore Her. She's cracked.

Or so innocent She thinks the assassin
Has Her in mind when he aims. What's death?

She thinks the hard-hats dream of Her swathed
In the flag. What's race or class or money?

She thinks the poets do it for Her
Out of reverence, and soldiers too for Her glory.

As to those other bitches, Justice
And Truth, they are cold and ugly. Who cares?

I tell Her: Here are two pills. For godsake,
Sleep. It's time for the last news.

80

In Miami fifty girls parade measurements by
For a crown. Beauty thinks that's great.

She thinks we can send home
The UN now that we've got Miss World.

I say it's vulgar. She laughs. I say there's something
Inhuman about it. She says sure.

And yawns and tells me: Get with your time,
And stretches and says: What lasts is style.

And now suddenly She wants to dance.
Where is Your social conscience, You whore?

I whisper this in Her ear as we dance.

SORRY

After the fifth beer,
Milwaukee softens, fine snow
Wafting me back to the hotel
Where the warmth of the lobby
Floats me up to my room.

I'm calling long distance now
To say: It's all right love, after all.
But am told the number has changed,
Sorry, unlisted—
Well, that sobers Milwaukee.

The windows look darkly out on stone,
And I've found another place to lose touch with.
Tomorrow in Boston, I'll call myself here
And they'll just have to say:
He's gone.

LETTER

I'm writing this to you
From two miles inside a Chinese painting
Called *Mountains After Rain.*

For a long time I too dreamed of money
In the pockets of love dining nightly
On power and Peking Duck.

I was called intimate first names
In silken rooms, and in public deferred to
As "The Master."

Exiled, I thought: "This is the end
Of the world," and it was, a narrow trail
Westering into the fog.

The painter wanted that intense green
Of autumn just before the world
Renounces itself.

This then is not death or happiness
But a long comfortable meditation
On the impossible.

So I write to prepare you for the next disappointment,
Its beauty, its loving art, and its need,
And for the disappointment after.

WASHING SOCKS

Penelope, old dear, you write
That all that keeps you sane these days
Is washing socks, faded socks,
And add: "For godsake, come on home."

I'm out here having adventures, sleeping
With goddesses, though sometimes I feel
Like a swine. I'm battling giant man-
Eating abstractions. I'm at sea.

There was the Island of Romance, the greener
Islands of Marx, of Freud, the misty
Isle of Zen and the volcanic Sartre.
And then there is plain old Ithaca.

You're bending over the tub, hearing
The kids bicker in the background, thinking
Of all the passes you passed up,
All for the owner of these faded socks.

And I will get there soon. War
Takes a long time, abstractions centuries
To escape, romance to wake from, and the sea
Itself is no friend to marriage.

I will come up the beach barefoot,
Grinning, and you'll make me sit right there
And put on those socks, smiling bitterly
Down because they no longer fit.

But for the kids, make the best of it.

PUMPERNICKEL

Feh! You call this pumpernickel,
This a political system, a living?
What do you call this? Forty years
Uncle Morris has been dreaming Russia.

The comrades there, snow on their whiskers, rub
Red hands by the hearth, its fire kindling their eyes
As they praise heroes, toast revolution
Sing love songs in tears, untranslatable.

Of late though, Uncle Morris is dreaming
Badly and considers a flight of fancy
To Israel. But its absence of snow chills him.
What do you do with a camel, an Arab?

So he waits his exile out like an unused alias
Of Trotsky, rocking a chair designed
In Ohio, watching the Fords go by
As he chews slowly like a man cursing.

JANE SEAGRIM'S PARTY

This calls for a toast. She hates
To admit it, but Jane is one hundred today
And reporters are coming by to watch
Her blow the candles out and ask,
Dearie, how, how did you do it
And how can we, who love speed,
Drink, cigars and have so deep
A sense of the tragic? And she will grin,
Exposing blackness on either side
Of her original stumpy canines and maybe
Wink who laid out three good husbands,
Receives postcards from her kids' kids
Having fun in another world
With people in it, can't even follow
TV to see the good life
In color—like two weeks in Hawaii—
She's missed, and is terrified of children
Who want, hugging, to break her bones,
Eats mush and drinks tea, thank you,
Won't be sampling her own cake,
And anyway the taste buds have all bloomed
And died long ago and it's shocking
To sit on the toilet and look down.

Nevertheless, one joy is left—
To pull, if she had it, from under her skirts,
A dainty pistol out and, right
In the middle of their disbelief,
Shoot these smartasses dead
Who thought this old life
Had no more to show them.

REVIVAL MEETING FOR
WHEELCHAIRS AND STRETCHERS

Don't tell him about the beauty of losing
Or about miracles. He has had bread
Turn to stone in his bowels, sewage
Back up to his eyes, his life wither out
From under him, except the pain.

Down from the hills, across the flatlands
He jerked and snorted, hauling into L.A.
Under a black sky through hostile traffic
And squatted, hearing on the radio Great Ideas
That would save him and didn't, so he spat and glared back.

Tell him instead of a free trip to the Hawaiian Hilton,
A tenth floor suite, meals served under silver
By small and selfless men, roses changed
Every day, a color TV, Jack Daniels,
And a girl who would do it for nothing but fun.

He would rise from the stretcher like pure spirit
Singing hallelujah, converted to a faith
You could hardly tell from indifference, a life
That never had to come down to the world again
Where the sick and the poor fight, crouching, over the dirt.

Meanwhile the sky gets blacker under his nails
And the prayers for salvation flame in his ears
Like curses. He has come all this way
To be saved and there's talk of sin, of cause
And effect, but he knows he's dying by sheer miracle.

GREAT

It's great to be miserable and know it—
Pascal. That's manhood: misery.
It's great. My dog Oliver
Is not great, nor the apple tree.

Pity them, lacking this aptitude
For being great like you and me,
Or my father who is even greater,
More prone to misery.

His ulcer tells him at three A.M.:
You are great, Jack, and his spine,
When he pulls on a sock, measures his greatness
In miles of glorifying pain.

Sometimes I catch in Oliver's eyes
A shade of something very like grief,
But no—my own reflection; and the apple?
How can it hurt to lose a leaf?

Let's get together and compare miseries;
It will be great, because whoever
Has most we'll give a prize—Pascal's
Jawbone or a day in the skull of Oliver.

THE PENANCE

This is the penance: a recurring dream,
This child running down the road, its mouth
A hole filled up with blackness, its little wings
Two flares of napalm and it runs toward you.

You can't yet hear its scream but know it's screaming,
Know if it can reach you, it will try to
Hug you and that napalm is contagious,
A deadly foreign plague for darker people.

Nothing can save you—voting, letters, marches—
So you close your eyes. A hundred years
It seems to take, the child getting nearer,
Bigger, maybe not so scared as furious.

Now you hear its scream—a supersonic
Jet-like whine that peels your skin off patch
By patch, and then the face is in your face,
Close as a lover's, eyes as bleak as bullets.

Then black-out till you wake forgetting all,
Forgetting him who felt the burning arms
Around him, but who can't, it seems, save any
Thing that matters though he knows what matters.

So this is the penance: a recurring dream
That you're awake and doing good, loving
The children, saving for their education
And your own retirement—till you close your eyes.

HAY FEVER

In the spread kingdom of Acacia
The April air is raining gold,
Sweet particles drenching the headlands,
Boiling up the river systems
Until, gasping for breath, the world
Is seen through a waste of tears, the word
Gargled in mounting waters.
                              Surplus
Of flowering, of fluids, of being
In the swollen season, bees sunk
Under its load, smothered
By the sheer joy of making.

In this flawed system, the face blossoms,
Praising by cough, sneeze
And the misery of itch and ugly red
The nonsense of God's blind plenty,
Saying: suffer this little evil.

In such waste is
The hope of children,
The stigma and lavish proof
Of love.

HONORABLE MENTION

It's some kind of little gray-leafed
Wild flower on the wind side
Of the dune and bent by habit
Hard away from the sea.

Between the great tides
And counter tides, its minute attention
Clutches down, grasping at the favor
Of indifferent rocks.

And after all the prizes are passed out,
Its yellow bloom seems futile,
Except to bees who also make a sweetness
Out of small desperation.

AUDIT

Listen. Wind hangs in the pine branches.
The year is done. There are certain things against you.
The lull is around the house, waiting.
But moss on the cold side of the bark is with you,
A jackrabbit frozen at the odor of fox is with you,
And a last apple, with a worm in it.
If you could see through the mist, a heaven of stars
And the granite under the dirt are perhaps with you.
When you close your book, its story will be with you too,
This plot of a traveler who against a sea came home,
His life his prize. If you listen minutely enough
Even the worm in the star, the fox in the rabbit's
Clenched heart are with you, though they seem hard companions.

On the north side of this thought, the moss is ready
To fend off the wind; or you breathe, and the wind is with you.

FROM
DEAR BLOOD

1980

GAP

This is the gap
for one butterfly to pass through,
a lucky break in the senseless green.

It's there by the grace of God,
who is I think the absence of a spider
at this particular time and place.

You may think He's the absence only
of leaves now dead or, more incredible yet,
the presence of the one butterfly.

WIDOWHOOD

It's as if the wife
of King Lear wandered onstage
after the play
and since there was no script
they had to hustle up
a few lines of pious resignation
to staunch the tears—
the cue for a heads-up exit,
while in the unlit alley outside,
its right rear door flung open,
the black Buick from the nursing home
snarled under the toe of a booted lackey.

OPPORTUNITY

We thought we owned the apple
having raised it simply
to bite at our pleasure.

But this worm
found it a sweet way
into its own ripeness.

That was a mouthful
of sour knowledge
for spitting out.

Could there be a higher purpose
that used us both
toward its own ripening?

Ha, say the dark seeds,
ha, and exult
to the core.

EVOLUTION

You've seen how it works —
backwards in huge silence.

So the cat's got your tongue but can't talk,
the butterfly your vagrant grace
without a reason, while your muffled heart
races the fox to its last hole.

And we who began as human, modeling
love for certain Italian Masters,
now slide by, low in shadow,
or freeze, hoping to be taken for stone.

YOURS TRULY

Sometimes a wild thing
will walk right out of the woods
into your hands
and you, thinking of something else,
kneel and receive it
as if it were yours to stroke
from the very first
and then it's gone,
the after-color of fox fading
into the woods and the woods
darkening shut behind it
while you stare down at spread hands
measuring an emptiness
nothing else can fill

and this is love
and this is a judgment.

CREED

Listening for reality,
I hear instead strange sounds—
far-off barking, wind or tide
sifting through pines, a soft spell
of mere breathing.

     My faith
without the least effort
has been in those things
from the very start
as my foot every step
of the way has believed in the ground.

HOLE

The mouse crawled through it,
the snake after him
and you're next.

Did you think
because Socrates went through
and Saint Francis
it was going to be bigger?

They also squeezed every hope
into its least possibility,
shedding layer after layer
to slide, tongue flicking,
into the rank darkness.

O yes,
the self is that small.

FAMILY CIRCLE

When I left Ithaca
for the great action
I was clean-cut, smartly
purposeful and nice
by inexperience.

I thought I'd be back soon
because the earth is flatly
a circle, but found,
though you want to go straight,
what survives is bent.

Well, here I am finally,
beat-up pilgrim to a homely shrine,
my bare rock and old woman
willing glumly to receive what I offer—
a scar and a tall story.

I see my son's eyes lift slyly
from his plate, asking what it was for—
struggle, shipwreck, and such lies.
It was for this, sonny, this:
my eating and your asking.

TENDRIL

Born for this world
you'll be tough as rope
five years from now
when we'll remember
the first maiden curl
reaching
delicately
out
for a blind feel,
and pity ourselves
gripped,
gripping,
to the death.

THE ELECTION

How did the stones vote
this time?

They voted for hardness
and few words

as the trees voted
for slow growth
upward and a shedding
of dead dependents.

And the men?

They voted against
themselves again
and for fire
which they thought they
could control,
fire
which voted for blackened stumps
and no more elections.

AT THE WELL

Does this water
taste of oil to you?

They say drink
what you don't use in the car.

Do these pipes
serving the wrong thirst
reach down to the wrong assumption
so pumping a septic mix
into the pitcher?

They say it's all a waste
anyhow
so accept it.

Do you feel bad
swallowing that?

They say this numbness
is life adapting to new conditions.

The numb parts of me
believe them.

COUP

That chair
isn't yours anymore.

Noon
when bells shed iron
on the dusty sleep of the poor
we took your chair.

The Republic
is now a wall
for you to die against
and (after a whitewash)
a background
for our smiles.

No hard feelings.

LAW AND ORDER

After the old gangster said
of a young revolutionary:
I could eat that bastard's
two eyeballs like cherries,
he added:
when I killed people
they asked for it.

No offense.

From
TO BE READ TO YOURSELF
IN A PUBLIC PLACE, JULY 4, 1976

1

If you start in loneliness
and buckskin.

If you cross rivers with no visible farther bank,
decades of hot grass,
cold uncut altitudes.

If you kill buffaloes
and braves for plausible reasons.

If you look out at the Pacific
and feel unsatisfied.

If you find gold—just like that—
under your feet.

What are you supposed
to do now?

Is America space merely to be crossed
over and over by loneliness
whose far edge, however lucky, is dissatisfaction?

Through iced hemlocks and snow a buck
still listens as though death were just hunting
enough to get through winter like a Cayuga.

As before we came,
as if we never arrived.

3

Through the thin hill fog
the young city across the Bay
is an amber nebula.

All possibilities await you there,
every disappointment
and your heart goes out.

Especially it goes out,
racing over the windy bridge,
to disappointment.

4

On the sink of the Golden Motel washroom
the water glass is swathed
in fresh sterile paper.

The Old World
doesn't care if a wall needs paint
or smells of piss.

Here it seems I've got to believe
no one ever lived (or died)
in this room.

6

It's a brand new morning
to rise, shower,
put on clean underwear,
start over again,
routinely reborn
as if Voltaire had never lived,
or Bismarck or Tolstoy.

What do you do
with this well-meaning idiot,
the American?

Nod and cheer him on.

Did you expect what began in hope
not to develop its habit
any more than a gray branch
gives up trying to thrust
its blind little horns into spring?

Nod and cheer me on.

8

I write you out of fear
and out of love.

Yesterday your granchildren discovered
in the playground a murder.

Under some kind of bush. It will change
their lives, how we can't tell.

They were playing after rain. You know—
clear sweet air and puddle-splash.

Police were professional, but ashamed,
wouldn't answer questions.

Last night was a new silence at dinner.
Crocuses grew on that very spot.

A sudden show of gold in spring.
It was just a young girl.

Stay well. The children asked to be remembered.
They're playing now out back.

I hear their cries.

9

There's too much to consecrate.

What the poor have done
to survive in all these exclusive riches.

What the old have done
to endure all this private newness.

What the intelligent have done
just to stay sane crossing pure mineral space.

What the small have done
not to be crushed under the shadow of redwoods.

What the good have done
to go on when all they get is a garbled echo for their trouble.

What couples have done
to love anyway after the end of credit.

What the lone brave has done
to go on dancing even while they built a shabby institution around
    him.

These huge stars they struggle under in America
and adore, the cold gorgeous star-system.

How they lose and persist anyway,
out to discover the New World.

It's this failure to be consecrated
and nevertheless persist.

To persist and to be consecrated.
Done. Done in the poor unprecedented doing.

LETTER

Dear Antigone,
after going over all the arguments
pro and con, I'm as divided as ever,
but when the last word dies away,
I know you're right.

Everybody does,
that's why Creon has to bury you
every time the state can't make children
obey the letters of the law
that don't spell love.

And that's why I stand here watching it all,
glad no one has asked me to help,
my littlest daughter's hand in mine,
her eyes looking up with a sad trust,
already forgiving.

KIND

I hadn't noticed
till a death took me outside
and left me there
that grass lifts so quietly
to catch everything
we drop and we drop
everything.

TO TRANSCEND THE CAT

1

Out of a half-
demolished church,
its chancel the clear sky,
we saw sparrows
flock suddenly up
startled as spirits
dissolving deep
into radiant vacancy.

2

Sparrow
is your basic bird.

He can't live
by intimations.

Where he flies
there's good reason.

When he sings
necessity keeps time.

3

One maple leaf remains
of summer—I try to let it be,
a lone survivor.

But can't. A thin stem
links it to a branch
distracted by sparrows
as I'm distracted
from onlyness as from
a last delusion.

4

Preston knows
Acer macrophyllum
as a common ornamental tree,
The Big Leaf Maple,
tolerant but preferring
moist sites for its fast rise
and shallow roots that support
the whole system
(including winged seeds)
under a compact crown.

Preston knows.

5

When branches glow
in the late sun
birds seem dark buds
of fire on a candelabrum
and the whole system
celebrates.
            Preston,
do you also celebrate?

6

Sparrow perched
on a warm bough
feels he was made
for this world
and so sings.

He's forgotten

his own strangeness.

It's his faith
to forget.

7

Fluttering at
the glass turret
of Mrs. Miller's feeder
(a column uplifted
to transcend the cat)
the hungry soul of sparrow
is reduced to pure
twittering want
the cat studies
in his enforced leisure.

8

I'm a student too.
I try to connect birds
with trees (and cats).

So far it's just theory.

9

Mr. Zane, eighty-two,
manages fifteen stairs
in twenty minutes, slower
than a sparrow's fall

to the landing below
where he stands
like an old stump
remembering.
It's our faith
to remember.

10

The chisel that gouged rot
out of the heartwood
left a shocked mouth,
a gasp of shadow.

Now the tree speaks
for itself. Now
it stands for itself.

11

Nevertheless
every time sparrow
settles on the maple
he creates the world
singing it up
from its dark origins
to a dome of light.

Who am I
not to accept creation
whatever it is?

CLOSURE

My mother died as though,
going out a door, she closed it
softly so it wouldn't disturb
my father watching TV.

Why fuss? Why make something
out of it? But isn't the habit
of life to make something
out of everything?

She knew that, but this once
refused, maybe because she saw
in that doorway at last death
wasn't a creature of habit.

HIEROGLYPH

I think the soul
is Egyptian
carved small on an old stone face
in a long parade of figures
some even bird-headed
all fixed and facing a far-off meaning
to be deciphered at last
by a brighter future.

Much is behind you
not to be known
and much ahead
of where you stand only for one true sound
(less maybe than a word)
before knowledge passes on.

Be ready,
be clear.

AND FINALLY

It's a plain table,
beech or alder,
the grain humbly confessing itself
through clear varnish.

The cup sitting alone
on its surface is cracked but good enough
to hold what winter requires
and a bent serviceable spoon.

One of the two chairs is for you
though both may be empty
when you arrive to find
a book lying beside the cup.

It's the very one
you always intended to read—
anywhere in it you turn
will be your story.

FROM
HOLDING PATTERNS

1982

THE UNDERSTANDING

We don't speak the same language
but by some miracle understand each other.
I hold up a pencil and say pencil
and you say yes, yes, pencil
and make signs of writing in the air
and the air becomes intelligible.

We don't need a translator to confuse us.
I look out at the sunset and say O
and you nod, yes, yes, yes
and maybe see the same vermilion
mingled with silver mingled with lemon,
cobalt with fire, earth with water.

You say perhaps we're speaking some
third language in a dream and it's all
illusion. We should pinch each other
to see if it's true. We pinch. It hurts.
We are nevertheless unconvinced.
We gossip. We abandon talk of the truth.

This becomes habit. We don't listen
anymore. We don't need to. I pinch you
now and then and can't remember why
and you cry out and we make up
and there are children around us like waves
tripping our feet. Do you understand?

I point to the sunset but you study the saucepan.
Yes, you say, I understand. The stringbeans
are about ready. Put out the wine.
I put out the wine. It doesn't matter
if it's not real. Language is just
music to live by anyway.

A MUSICAL OFFERING

Bach is spreading softly down
from the small house with one lit window
halfway up the hill.

I'm merely passing but stop to listen
with head bowed as one who receives the overflow
of another man's blessing.

It reminds me that the poor still wait
out in the rain, silently bearing their lives
like a burden of useless wings,

and that long dead stars send
waves of light out to the edge of darkness
though no one may ever see,

and that Bach himself, late and alone,
laying aside his towering wig, must
sometimes have stared blindly
into the candle.

MEADOW FOAM

Woe to them that are consoled. . . .
—Marie Lenéru

The afternoon
hundreds of blackbirds
suddenly sprang up
out of the cedars of the cemetery
he felt, for Christ's sake,
a vision had been vouchsafed
the wrong man again,
as in that dry Mexican spring
when one sunset slowly spread
like a vast pang for the loss
of a whole heaven of light,
which he resented, knowing
that dust makes gorgeous
the banal glow of dying suns,
dust, our own poor medium,
or on that cold day in Normandy
when he alone met Evil,
a German tank half in a ditch
beside the road, its black cross
scorched, its long gun pointed
blindly at the milky sky,
and eastward, brown smoke
on the ghostly horizon, signaling
a great work in progress
of which he was a part but not
a part, or on that summer night
seated under constellations
of lit crystal when everyone

seemed moved together inward
by one concentric music, and then
applause fading into departure
like a tide going out
or exile into the dark
of yourself, and now this big
stagey uprush and whisper of flight,
a poor man's phoenix dissolving
before his very eyes, and he
stupidly as ever
disappointed and disappointed
with much else—"disappointed,"
a word pronounced like falling
down stairs, and here he was
at the bottom, unhurt, perhaps
a little stunned, grateful
for small bruises and—disappointed
because wars, elections, views
of the Alps, of skyscrapers
and Rembrandts promised more,
and these flagrant visions
that seem to hint of Great Doings
behind the masks of mere light
and shadow, behind flesh (dust
again) and its best wishes, and here
he stood looking for a word
that would let him be—say, "reconciled,"
spoken with good-humored sadness
that made him feel like the ghost
of himself, one of the liberal dead
ready to accept anything almost,

even love, another distraction
from blackbirds and far-off figures
of glory, and without thinking
he turned to the woman beside him,
slender, tall almost
as he, a lilac scarf
around her gray hair that hung
in thin bangs across her forehead,
and the same gray eyes he'd watched
this morning as she studied her face
in the mirror, eyes not warmly open
as now, but narrowed, calculating
as a painter's, working only with flesh,
shadow, light, and a few pastels
to make a decent likeness
of her best self, the one
that accepted what was there
and what was not, seeing herself
maybe as simply the exposed negative
of a woman long gone
in the mirror, the lost and real one
he loved, as she herself loved
the far-off man whose decent likeness
she now smiled at, reconciled
and disappointed and there's your love
for you, the fine art of charity
and tact, of noticing and not
noticing, for example, people,
the world, or little scenes in it
like the modest arrangement of cedars
out there, a good picture
of middle-class composure,

their shade obscuring gravestones,
names, dates, woes of the flesh,
hopes, disappointed love,
and making death into a tame
old pasture missing only
its pious white mare and her
sleepy aura of flies, or making
life a kind of exclusive club
for self-pity, civil doubt,
and guilt, a private place to think
occasionally of those excluded—
beggars on Bombay streets asking
for nothing more than another day
like the last, black-eyed children
watching enemy jets scream in
over low white buildings,
his neighbor, a strong old man
with a bad heart, and so on
till he cried (without moving
his lips), "Not this, not this!"—
but what then, what? and was answered
by his own heart beating hard
as though caught sleeping on duty,
the same old faithful pump
fifty-eight years serving it knew
not what, perhaps the vague hunger
they used to call the soul,
a sort of dumb cry and flutter
in the dark or cave of dreams,
unique all right, but over
the long haul nothing special,
nothing to interest the Great Powers

of Light and Darkness, yet knowing
itself caged in the wrong world,
trying hard to remember back
to some translucent first cause
or ahead to a radiant last one
but always getting stuck in details,
say, the manner in which light
(lower-case illumination)
defines a soft curve of flesh
out of mere shadow to become
a whole strange dependable face
in the chill frame of pure silver,
or the way common blackbirds crash
into an almost acceptable scene
to distract the comfortably disappointed
from their little faith,
or even simpler, as when she knelt
last Saturday morning by the sea,
knelt at what he hadn't noticed
just at his feet, a white surprise
or wild flower out of its place,
time, maybe even its world,
knelt of a sudden and said softly
over it its local name
which he had forgotten till now, and now
repeated like an unanswerable prayer
for all things that must stand for themselves,
things plain to the vision—
repeated without moving his lips,
"meadow-foam, oh meadow-foam,
of course," and that would have to do.

TABLE TALK

Therefore, this first kind of grace,
common to all, is seldom called grace.
—Erasmus

She was just about to say,
through the candles and over the wine,
with the oak table and so much else
between them, that distance
was no less fine an invention
than the wheel, but didn't
because his smile was too far off,
so asked softly instead: Are you there?
and knew, though he lifted his glass
to her, he wasn't, but somewhere back
in himself alone with something dearer
to him than any woman now,
what—for modesty—he called
his disappointment, that is, failure,
which these days left her much
to herself to decide just who
she was after all these years
typecast as daughter, wife, mother,
double agent in the lost war
of the sexes, or someone yet to meet,
like the skeleton lady who wore *her* rings
in the mirror of a bad dream, or even
the limber unbespoken girl
she had betrayed centuries ago,
the same happy bird-boned fool
who used to float up through wild flowers
under pure wind music overhead
to reach a vision of the Bay below
where light was a shatter of green brilliants
so fierce she had to turn aside
and found there, like a consolation,

the pasture easing down at her left,
made comely by the pious grazing
of one dusty old roan and,
O Lord, gravity seemed with her then,
and when *he* arrived on the crest,
magnetism and also—touching—
electricity, and later darkness
seemed only an ample room for whatever
love, conjuring with small lights
or stars, could conceive in the sweet silence
of birds and all she had to do
was stretch out her hand and . . .
here she was now as though flushed
from a leafy drowse in which someone
had invented distance and it was real,
a kind of exile where she felt herself
diminished and solitary, observed
by an eye far off and detached
and nothing to do but sadly take
her helpmate's hand and walk off
into the thorns and thistles
and here they were finally, all
but alone—good gray tenants
of a nicely appointed future, complete
with this intimate candle fiction,
these artful wine-dark shadows
which softened disappointment and made
waiting for unthinkable death (she blushed
at that) a comfort that left him
the leisure to stare, as he did now,
right through flesh and blood
as though something waited further on,

131

some (of course) modest grail hidden
behind a misty door ahead, or perhaps
he saw nothing or the worser nothing
beyond nothing, or perhaps distance
was for him a place you were duty-
bound to visit from time to time,
like the cemetery they strolled
this afternoon to call on old friends
and were both shaken by a wild upflutter
of blackbirds in their hundreds
that left him gaping at the radiant void
of their absence (much, she thought, like a cow
gazing rapt at a spot where something
strange had passed) and she wanted to take
his hand—helpmate, old companion—
and tell him she also could see
immense prospects narrowed to one
beige accoustical tile
of an institutional ceiling, and so
to trust neither in visions nor dreams,
but in faithful seeing or trying to see
just what was there or almost there
(things flapped off so fast), as one
absolute time she saw, as she looked
over the water below, saw and accepted,
perhaps a mile out, a small
white sail leaning far over
the green dissonant swells, folding
the wind to its own purpose
like a sheer garment, not hers
and not her purpose but near enough

to see the free uses of grace
and the fair chance of such small
impromptu choices as sailors are given,
though it was now he who leaned forward
and asked: Are you there? and she wanted to add
that this woman or disappointment
across the table from him and like him,
was an outlandish specimen, creature
from alien space or long distance
arrived to discover what was human
or left after the romance of visions,
dreams, failure, and common
household pain, but answered instead
unsmiling: Yes, I'm here (where else
on earth could she be!) and lifted her glass.

NEAR THINGS

The wild blackberries I gathered that morning
when the world seemed on the lit verge
of some especially lovable form
were still bitter. You smiled anyway.
It was your second-best smile,
the one reserved for making do
with things as they are, and we did.

And as the day slowly ripened,
everything we saw or touched
touched us in consolation
for a sweetness we never had—and it was good.
That night the stars were simply
beyond reach and we ignored them
for this world, dark as it was.

TOAST

There was a woman in Ithaca
who cried softly all night
in the next room and helpless
I fell in love with her under the blanket
of snow that settled on all the roofs
of the town, filling up
every dark depression.

Next morning
in the motel coffee shop
I studied the made-up faces
of women. Was it the middle-aged blonde
who kidded the waitress
or the young brunette lifting
her cup like a toast?

Love, whoever you are,
your courage was my companion
for many cold towns
after the betrayal of Ithaca,
and when I order coffee
in a strange place, still
I say, lifting, this is for you.

CONVERSATION PIECE

Of late I've been talking to my shadow
more and more. Why not? He's read Pascal
and Buber. He's lain awake nights thinking
through the Great Questions, above all
the existence of the soul, which you and I
had thought a dead issue. He's not so sure.

Simensky, I say (that's his name), you're
a reader, a philosopher, so tell me—when
the lights go out, when all that's left is fear,
a snuffle like horses, the sudden silence of crickets,
when footsteps walk into the middle of sleep
and stop as if in thought, what then are dreams? Dreams?

Simensky, your silence on this matter suggests
that experience, this bare handful of water,
sometimes sweet, sometimes stale, matches
my thirst so well, that I may really be meant
for this world, period. The rest is—oh—
shadow calling out to shadow, absence to absence.

We go on like this until it's dark
when my mooning lamp gives Simensky
an especially soft look as though he wanted
to console me for being so obscure. Simensky,
I whisper, this breathing, is it the truth,
the whole truth? He nods and reaches for the bottle.

THAT THE UNEXAMINED LIFE
IS NOT WORTH LIVING

So, butterfly,
you and the leaf you sit on—
bronze idling on bronze—
are just going to have to die
without knowing how pretty
and pointless your lives are.

We humans, however,
understand the backward grace
of flight and fall, and also
understand the pity
of not knowing, and also
the pity of knowing.

NEWS FROM THE LOW COUNTRY

Down where the stone's cold shadow
moves on the calm face of ditchwater
everyone tells the truth, a small thing
but it makes being here like nothing else—
no love quite like hunger,
no hue like gray, no music like breathing,
no kindness so tender as the soft
reception of a homeless leaf.

MORNING SONG

Dreaming the actual world,
I saw you again last night,
the moon turning your dark hair
its own color, your face the face
of my first girl, a fantasy
full of bitterness and hope,
nothing on earth more beautiful.

If they ask who you are, I'll say,
sister of death, cold daughter
of wishes only come true
in the risen Atlantis of sleep, and yet
most constant of all, waiting
at the missed stations ahead, patient
as love, for what I'll never be.

HOLDING PATTERN

—for Somebody's Old Aunt

A dream: she is learning to fly
without wings. Well, nonsense,
but what isn't these days?—
thus when the mocking bird
wakes her (never so fine
in its mocking as now and never
so much itself either),
she lies there and listens unmoved
by its intimation of something
rarer than it, a high-toned
golden nightingale
from a Chinese fairy tale
where there is no time
like the present, no arches
fallen, joints inflamed,
no cold oatmeal to rise to,
no need to escape
by the same street to the same
park to the same bench,
to waste the day in the shadow
of shaky elm leaves
stained with stale atoms
of smoke, to be cooed at
by pigeons, chirped at by her own
gray kind, and, home again,
cackled or crowed over
by her ruffled niece, and served
(whatever they call it) oatmeal,
and then to outwait night,
straining her watery glasses
over some birdbrained romance,
and then to sleep, to dream,

perchance to fly, and fall
back into the world
only to wonder if rising
again is not merely
to yield to the bad habit
of hope, but now hears
the mocking bird insist
with its whole gray soul
that morning calls for some
sort of celebration,
even if what you sing
is someone else's solo,
a mocking anthem of joy
which demands that she rise again,
wingless and doubtful as ever,
rise and warily open
the blinds expecting as ever
to find only what's there
and sees, like a shy vision,
that at least the anxiety
of the poplars is no longer
her anxiety, that the blue
and innocent emptiness of the sky
is not her emptiness
and so (humming without knowing
she hums) washes her body,
removing from it what wastes
she can, robes herself
in something clean and simple,
then wambles down the stairs,
flat step by flat step,
to honor the oatmeal with honey

and abide the bitterness
in the plucked souls of her kin,
caged as she is in the wrong
and only life as only
she among them knows,
now entering the kitchen
warm as a new-laid egg,
the first human, the first
always to rise, thinking
that this dream, stranger
than all, will soon be over,
but I'm having it now,
so it's mine, or my making
or mocking, homely bird,
poor man's nightingale,
and lifts like a toast the first
sweet adequate mouthful.

SICK LEAVE

—for Bill Brandt

Now there's nothing in this world
that only you can set right—your roses
will blossom without you, your love be made,
your own job done and maybe better.

This is a new kind of freedom, a heart
full of panic like canaries uncaged
by error into a great failure
of light and blue breathtaking chance.

JUBILEE

Listen—she's coming now
through the long sigh of a bus door,
through the weepy gusts
of November, up the twilight boredom
of twenty-seven (count them) steps,
and now into the room where the light
suddenly remembers things
just as they were this morning,
though lonelier perhaps
and that could be why she flings
her hood back as if in defiance
and, muttering, peels off her raincoat
like an old skin, hanging it high
to shed the tears she won't,
and why she charges the kitchen,
surprising the absence out of it,
to start the kettle heating,
and only then comes back out to drop
with a sigh into the giving
old armchair where bitterly
she recalls she's stopped smoking
again so, damn it, there's nothing
to do before she warms the leftovers
but quietly be
here between the day's petty rages
still pecking in her skull
like a typewriter, and the night's
long well-read solitude yet to come,
for she expects no one and hasn't
for thirty years since she packed
her girlhood in the trunk
with all the innocent trash of memory
and her mother's wedding dress,
which is only to say

144

she trails neither glory
nor dust behind her and owes the future
nothing but next month's rent
so she can sit in the calm pasture
of this moment and summon back,
atom by weary atom,
her scattered self into that simple composure
which is also the wholeness or beauty
of otherwise homely queens
in their full power, the very thing
we've been waiting here
to tell her all this time,
but in her kingdom have no more mouth
for it than ghosts and anyhow
she doesn't believe in ghosts,
only in what remains after the trunk
is locked, which for her, it seems,
is a chronic procession of small erasable choices,
like being just or kind
from one faithless moment to the next,
choices you wouldn't notice
unless you cared to,
and now, changing
into a blowsy red robe,
she hears the kettle commence
its hysterical jubilee
and by God thinks
tonight she'll have brandy before sleep,
the imported kind that begets
such smooth experienced fire
out of mere sweetness and time,
to be served in her place only
on proud occasions of state.

SOLEMN MUSIC

Especially in rain my faith
is with women talking on the other side
of a wall, sometimes low and in sorrow,
sometimes laughing without reason,
a music almost becoming words.

Of course, I'd rather believe
like you in the long green trill
of a bird, or the root mystery
of a dead tree that can blossom
a man, or simply in the facts.

But rain persuades me that nothing
will last but the low voices of women
reciting sorrow inside, hymning
unreasonable joy while they wait for me
to enter and join their secret devotions.

THE SERVANT OF STARS

When she took the whiskey sours out
of his hands, Dawn, the new
cocktail waitress, whispered to Jack,
the aloof bartender, that he looked
a lot like Humphrey Bogart, his back
to the world, and frowning as though distracted
by the smoky violet mirror
that spanned the whole length of the bar
like a cold and darkling window on
to space in which faint constellations
with common names like Mary, Bud,
and Doc were composed of little lights
you may have thought were only human—
glint of eyes leaning forward
to drink, flash of a wedding band,
gleam of an earring, cigar glow—
a galaxy Jack could now observe
like some alien disguised as one
of *them*, say Humphrey Bogart, so
that when he turns to face the world
things are not the same, flushed
with a dim radiance that fringes
even the same old stunts:
Bud's sadness that held out
to the fifth Scotch, Mary's refusal
to take money for what she swears
is love, Doc's boyish grin
while his bony hand squeezes the throat
of his glass, and finally Jack himself,
his heart beating from sheer habit,
his hairpiece turning gray with worry,

his wife lost, taking with her
hope like the child they never had,
and here he is again suddenly
feeling—what? Space Sickness,
or maybe Space-Time Sickness,
a queasy passion to tell them all
the terrible news of desolation,
of black distances that no one
can ever cross, and how they drink
their own pity . . . but instead
he swabs the bar, pretending to wait
for the next order, pretending to be
Humphrey Bogart coolly noting
Dawn move off across the room
on brave skittish legs ready
to take a long run at time,
awkward and graceful both, as only
the young can be, her brown hair
lambent as candle light, her eyes,
turning back to him, him,
encouraging she knows not what—
the wrong man, poor double
for a dead star, himself simply
a poor double for something no one
ever saw, and now—what's this?—
Jack smiles at her a little
idiot smile the mirror cannot
see but the bar can, glaring
darkly up with a different version
of his face as though the heart
of wood opened to show him still

another secret self to hide from,
and he buries it below the rag
and vows never to ask which one
is real, if any is, and vows
further to do his job as if
that were all and composes himself
into the man he has to be,
a constellation of aches, rages
and fears, and this trifling skill,
all which answer to one name,
meaningless if said like a mantra
over and over, and yet, said once,
said only once a certain way . . .
O Jack, no more of that. Pity
but not love, drink but never
hope in this desolation. Still
(remembering her glance across
the whole length of the long room),
still there could be more to it
than *that*, something here unworldly
and clean that makes him stare out
over the bar as if at nothing,
but that's all right—no one, not
even she, notices because
these stars are so remote and blind.

HELLO AGAIN

In every greeting a final goodbye is said.
That's why my hand fits so comfortably in yours
and why my eyes from the very first glance
have never stopped asking yours: when,
how, and for what good reason?

Every parting is a rehearsal for the last.
That's why you call up the stairs a second time
to tell me that this one is just for practice,
that you'll be back soon with cigarettes
and a newspaper full of fresh disaster.

Every life is an example of what to hope for.
That's why each morning the mirror is studied
with such dumb devotion like a page of scripture,
and why every new face is commentary
on the old testament of our own.

THE CHOSEN

One morning a whole people
can wake up with nothing to do.
They look around fulfilled
and utterly without interest
at the promised land.

They stand listening before bushes
or incredulously tap rocks,
but the answer is always an echo
of their own making
or plain thirst.

Someone remembers to shout a command.
The women slowly get breakfast,
the men face outward,
searching the far dust,
looking for trouble.

EXPLANATION

When you said it wasn't my fault
but something in you that you couldn't explain
I knew you were already a memory
I had of a girl who stood at the window
looking out on the lost freedom of distance.

All that remains is a white blouse
in the closet, like a schoolgirl who can't explain
why she wants to be left alone,
or like a younger sister hiding
from the predestined failure of grown-ups.

I wish I could comfort her with flowers
or a future full of the sweets she thinks
we've cruelly withheld, but it's you she needs,
you, to explain what it's like to be absent,
to be a memory that can't explain.

THE FOURTH DIMENSION

Some part of us lives
always in the fourth dimension,
the invisible part
which can pass through walls,
falls hopelessly in love with light
and asks us in bad dreams
what touching is like.

This is not the soul
or anything that God made,
only the imperfection or wonder
of something that can't be touched.
It looks out of Einstein's eyes
as innocence or sorrow
for a time never to be lived in.

THE SCROLL

In this sleep an old Chinese,
thin as a willow leaf, drifts
into his misty hut.

We're with him now
as he sits at a small table.
We're the pain in his lower back,

the headache through which he sees
the scroll, the cold hand
unrolling it slowly.

We read the poem
he has brushed there, our own exile
elegantly set down.

We think of the waterfall,
the white vein on the far-off
blue cliff face,

of pines dripping, of the brown river
and the small boat tied
in its reeds. Listen.

We're going to cry
but pour ourselves a cup
of wine instead.

We think reality
is only the pain and the cold,
and wake up

cold, hurting in the same
old places, our dream
still with us.

SO?

So you aren't Tolstoy or Saint Francis
or even a well-known singer
of popular songs and will never read Greek
or speak French fluently,
will never see something no one else
has seen before through a lens
or with the naked eye.

You've been given just the one life
in this world that matters
and upon which every other life
somehow depends as long as you live,
and also given the costly gifts of hunger,
choice, and pain with which to raise
a modest shrine to meaning.

SPIRIT

I'm thinking now of something
sighted once, maybe,
on the gleaming floor
of January: a small creature
wary under fir branches,
every breath pulsing
its whole body like a shudder,
its purpose so plain and mysterious
you could stare all these years
and see only how suspect
was your first and surprised view
of the thing (whatever it was)
as a sorry sight, because
surely it filled its moment
as warmth fills anything
that wholly contains it, as joy
flutters unreasonably
in the same brutal cage
where the heart beats
merely to keep time.

WAITING ROOM ONLY

Death has a younger brother
who hates his success.
There are nineteen cases
coming for the doctor today
not counting himself and his nurse
whose impatient red hair
just won't stay pinned
under a sterile cap
so she has to brush back
a little flame from her eyes
as she begins in a voice
flat as Kansas
to toll each afflicted name
at its appointed hour
beginning with Mr. Bailey
who limps up ramshackled
in faded tans, a smile
on his baggy face, pocked
as a target, and you may now recall
(if you're the doctor and you are)
that this too was born
of woman, come forth like a flower
to be cut down at last
but until then to be treated
as though a life could go on
forever if only you keep
at it, as he keeps
at it, breath after breath,
hauling himself here
like a sack to be looked into,
though the first thing to fly out
is the mercy bird hope,
a white flutter around

157

your head that you have to ignore
listening to the old heart
do its job, as Bailey
did his fifty years
faithful as an ox marching
through mud, up one row,
down another and you want
to ask why, why and what
is it to be human, to be
faithful, marching blindly,
or, as you do now,
to listen, tap, feel,
and even think suddenly
of a sick old elm
cut down, but its stump
this spring anyhow
blindly shooting at the sun
dozens of green saplings—
stupid that you should feel
this clear defiance a witness
for your own dumb kind,
for Mr. Bailey smiling
among the ashes and dust
when he might be demanding why,
why of his miserable comforter,
but waits, patient as a hireling
for a petty wage, this prescription
for local pain, and, grateful,
departs, leaving the nurse
alone with you a moment—
that burning strand almost
enough to make you forget
autopsies of what someone

loved too little or much,
or does its defiance remind you
of such half-witted transgressions
against necessity
and time, as the gladness
of Mr. Bailey, the passion
of a blind stump, testimony
you can't credit but is yet
hurtfully real, as she summons
(brushing a little fire
from her eyes) the next affliction
and you know then that the time
is already lost and has been
from the first hour and yet
you go on listening, feeling,
even thinking between
their troubles of one refusal
after another to give in,
as your patients refuse, however,
meekly they enter and go,
as the elm refuses, coming
to light again, as you also
refuse to hate yourself now
for being of this kind,
miserable but unrepentant
among the ashes and dust,
getting set for the next grief,
jealous as a lover
for the least sign of life,
defeated into gladness
by one little fallen strand
of red hair or fiery
heartstopping refusal.

159

THE SOUNDINGS

A freight train rattles and jars through sleep
in the cold grayness just before dawn
and I come to wild attention like a drowsy engineer
on the last of his shift, hauling darkness
behind him car after empty car and see
ahead the small lights of the city hiding
among them the last station of this run
and suddenly, alone with a present so pure
and moving, I reach over and sound the whistle
once and again and again like a great conch shell
pronouncing a solitary exaltation
there's no response to, except perhaps the sun.

PITT POETRY SERIES
Ed Ochester, General Editor

Dannie Abse, *Collected Poems*
Claribel Alegría, *Flowers from the Volcano*
Jon Anderson, *Death and Friends*
Jon Anderson, *In Sepia*
Jon Anderson, *Looking for Jonathan*
John Balaban, *After Our War*
Michael Benedikt, *The Badminton at Great Barrington; Or, Gustave Mahler & the Chattanooga Choo-Choo*
Michael Burkard, *Ruby for Grief*
Kathy Callaway, *Heart of the Garfish*
Siv Cedering, *Letters from the Floating World*
Lorna Dee Cervantes, *Emplumada*
Robert Coles, *A Festering Sweetness: Poems of American People*
Leo Connellan, *First Selected Poems*
Kate Daniels, *The White Wave*
Norman Dubie, *Alehouse Sonnets*
Stuart Dybek, *Brass Knuckles*
Odysseus Elytis, *The Axion Esti*
John Engels, *Blood Mountain*
Brendan Galvin, *The Minutes No One Owns*
Brendan Galvin, *No Time for Good Reasons*
Gary Gildner, *Blue Like the Heavens: New & Selected Poems*
Gary Gildner, *Digging for Indians*
Gary Gildner, *First Practice*
Gary Gildner, *Nails*
Gary Gildner, *The Runner*
Bruce Guernsey, *January Thaw*
Mark Halperin, *Backroads*
Michael S. Harper, *Song: I Want a Witness*
John Hart, *The Climbers*
Gwen Head, *Special Effects*
Gwen Head, *The Ten Thousandth Night*
Milne Holton and Graham W. Reid, eds., *Reading the Ashes: An Anthology of the Poetry of Modern Macedonia*
Milne Holton and Paul Vangelisti, eds., *The New Polish Poetry: A Bilingual Collection*
David Huddle, *Paper Boy*
Lawrence Joseph, *Shouting at No One*
Shirley Kaufman, *From One Life to Another*
Shirley Kaufman, *Gold Country*

Ted Kooser, *One World at a Time*
Ted Kooser, *Sure Signs: New and Selected Poems*
Larry Levis, *Winter Stars*
Larry Levis, *Wrecking Crew*
Robert Louthan, *Living in Code*
Tom Lowenstein, tr., *Eskimo Poems from Canada and Greenland*
Archibald MacLeish, *The Great American Fourth of July Parade*
Peter Meinke, *Trying to Surprise God*
Judith Minty, *In the Presence of Mothers*
Carol Muske, *Camouflage*
Carol Muske, *Wyndmere*
Leonard Nathan, *Carrying On: New & Selected Poems*
Leonard Nathan, *Dear Blood*
Leonard Nathan, *Holding Patterns*
Kathleen Norris, *The Middle of the World*
Sharon Olds, *Satan Says*
Greg Pape, *Black Branches*
Greg Pape, *Border Crossings*
James Reiss, *Express*
Ed Roberson, *Etai-Eken*
Eugene Ruggles, *The Lifeguard in the Snow*
Dennis Scott, *Uncle Time*
Herbert Scott, *Groceries*
Richard Shelton, *Of All the Dirty Words*
Richard Shelton, *Selected Poems, 1969-1981*
Richard Shelton, *You Can't Have Everything*
Arthur Smith, *Elegy on Independence Day*
Gary Soto, *Black Hair*
Gary Soto, *The Elements of San Joaquin*
Gary Soto, *The Tale of Sunlight*
Gary Soto, *Where Sparrows Work Hard*
Tomas Tranströmer, *Windows & Stones: Selected Poems*
Chase Twichell, *Northern Spy*
Constance Urdang, *The Lone Woman and Others*
Constance Urdang, *Only the World*
Ronald Wallace, *Tunes for Bears to Dance To*
Cary Waterman, *The Salamander Migration and Other Poems*
Bruce Weigl, *A Romance*
David P. Young, *The Names of a Hare in English*
Paul Zimmer, *Family Reunion: Selected and New Poems*